To f

GW01003218

Single Broke Female:

Poetry Collection

Zarina Macha

May someday this be
more accurately titled
'married rich female.'

Yours now & forever,

Zee xxxx

For Louisa Le Marchand and Gill Swan, with love and gratitude

Also thanks to George RR Martin for inspiring me with his magic of ice and fire, and Stephen King for helping me fight the deadlights

Also by Zarina Macha:

Fiction

Every Last Psycho: A Collection of Two Novellas

Anne

Poetry

Art is a Waste of Time: Poetry Collection

Author's Note

I would like to thank everyone so far for purchasing my debut poetry collection *Art is a Waste of Time*. Those poems are compiled over several years hence my decision to put the dates on all of them. I do go back and edit my poems later on, but this involves cutting unnecessary words or correcting tenses rather than changing the work as a whole. (The main essence of the poem remains unchanged hence I see no reason to include the editorial date.)

I haven't dated most of these as the majority were written in 2018 and 2019 and so capture a lot from that time period. There are clear themes woven throughout this collection hence why I have carefully arranged the order as opposed to listing them alphabetically.

I hope you enjoy it and gain something from it.

Contents

Blonde Beauty
Three Sisters
Down Under
I Don't Know
One Hundred and One Damnations
Recovery is Complicated
Life Sentence
Faith
To Thine Own Self
It Just Is
Red

Single Broke Female

Single Broke Female
     Looking to Share
         Rent and Bed.

         Non-Smoking
    Kind Man
      Preferred.

Contact allie jones if interested.

A Writer

A writer observes
she watches the world and writes every leaf
every sigh of a tree blowing in the wind
she listens.

Men tell her their woes
from tomcats to toads
they weave their weeps into her ears
she listens.

Fathers hang, mothers perish
partners cruelly plunge their seed
into bodies of unwilling lovers
while the child watches, unblinking
wondering why mummy and daddy aren't friends
meanwhile, the writer's globe spins dizzy
she listens.

Lovers fight and bite their claws
deep into hearts of fire
ladies scream, men storm and slam
the doors by which they came through
taking half of what they had
hoping their kids will see them through the window
aches for justice to chime the bells
of law and order
meanwhile, the writer stops to stare
she listens.

Swing right, swing left
swing and shake it all about
Ring red or ring blue
tootle-oo, fuck you
cry the many
(or the few)
watch the world burn, it's my turn
the mob waves its burning torch
the other lashes out frozen ice

merging winter winds with spring dreams
is either wrong or right? Who knows
the writer simply sees both sides
she listens.

In the end, the world will burn
stake your claim and be crowned queen of the ashes
when the world has crumbled and charred to a crisp
underneath all that's come and dipped
the writer shall stand, pen in hand,
for two swords create death while two pens breathe life
into a land before time
remembering sons of yours and mine
and daughters that sat, with pens in hand
who listened.

Misery (stream of consciousness)

The mind

        often wonders itself to misery

                        the worst

        time being at night

when all is still and nought does stir.

      When all is quiet

                   the mind finds itself seeping

        into

        twisted
        gnarled
        thoughts of doom and gloom
        anger and frustration.

A brilliant, quick-witted mind that does not mean to dwell on
despair

      that would not if it could not

but insomniac-ridden with no sheen of entertainment

           it is cast to lie until

                   morning

brings the fragments of the night

           before the light.

January 2016

Blocked out of Heaven

Hal's screen sneers obscene
At my frantic desperation.
Despite all best efforts, silent hisses
Pound their way into neurons
Fingers and head disconnect.

Blank. Words appear then stop.
'What next?' whispers Hal, sniggering
He stifles a laugh, I swallow my pride
The story refuses to budge.

'It won't write itself, you know.
Distract all you want
Social media,
Scribe metrical composition
This book remains unfinished.'

Hal sits, bright eyed,
Letters and numbers aching to be pressed.
Yet no formula stands to wait for me
To chop and mould this tale.

Trouble

Shaking, hands trembling; barely grips the pen
Burning ache in my chest rippling
Like pink acid.

His name falls on my lips – sweet kiss
Once again I'm accursed
With this infliction of a man's caress.

Why him? I wonder. *Why me?*
Cupid, why do this to me?
Just as she dragged herself out
You pulled her right back in.

A single crumb of hope shattered to bile
Like the food in my stomach refusing to
Curdle and
Distil
patiently in time.

I tried to run, no more mistakes
Yet another takes my breath away
Now I'm in trouble, again

Tried to close heaven's door,
Keep honey sweet sparkles away.
But it pushed too hard, captivating me
Its charms are unstoppable

Why do this to me, little cherub?
At least the arrow shot his head too
But minutes count down till time
Evaporates and forms a dry ocean

Moisture is soft at first,
Seems like the tide waves in
But when the glare of truth beams down, it fades
Leaving nothing but disappointed sand.

I tried to remain in the sand
But the tide of desire returned
Its only a matter of time
Before the tide sets out again.

'Enjoy the water!' they cry
'Lap it up and let it flow!'
Our bodies are mostly water
So why do I feel like stone?

I tried to steer clear of trouble
But it bit me on the toe
The purrs of the singing tomcat
Refuse to let me go

How much more disappointment
Can a heart of fire take?
All this trouble I am in
For want of finding a mate.

I should run fast, run now
For sure I have made a mistake
Before the tide evaporates
And I am left
Stranded in dreams and dust.

But no matter how hard I try
This poorly formed pink cloud
Remains fuzzy and stubborn
Refusing to part without a ray of sun.

Inside Man

Cream melts with caramel
Softly licking its way through butter
To form legs and limbs

Touch me, gently
I ache to be stroked
Up and down these walls

They shake and tremble, filling with water
Hold me and never let go
Your body is a delicious fruit
And I am the seed inside of you.

Hot kisses on my neck
Gasps echo from your windpipe
Shudders of pleasure ripple and glimmer
Tingles from toes to temple

Inside man the world stops
Inside man the washing machine
Spinning among my neurons
Is quiet.

Inside man I am two people
Two bodies merging.
Gently now, let's ride slow
There's no need to rush.

My Lover

Taste him in my mouth
His tongue quickens my pulse
Shooting all over tiny strands of hair
They prickle and stiffen like his glands

Drown in me baby
Ride the black horse
Mount and glide
Swiftly, then slowly,
Up and down
Trembles quake within us both

He climbs upon my saddle
Stroking the mare
This soft mane of hair
Then he straps in
Getting his strap on
The horse howls when it's ridden

Heat melts from his flesh
Like butter sizzling on a frying pan
Soft white pancake flesh
Tastes delicious, baby drink me
Till you squirt it out

Ride the dragon baby, ride the black horse
My lover
Your voice is music through my soul
He is a dream come true, a wish upon a star
But will he truly be mine?
Or will my hopes fall then
Crash and burn to Dante's inferno.

Lover, don't break me
For although I look stable
My skin may smash
If you're not there to catch me.

I'm Stupid

Stupid red-headed flower
Dancing stupid siren dreams
Just a stupid little girl
Surrounded by liars

They're all liars in the capital
And they're so much better than me
My stupidity runs from London to Cambridge
Tricking down the riverlands

Call me Lady Snow
For there is nothing I know.
If nothing is to be known
Then is nothing still something?
Who knows.

Stupidly I clap and run
Up and down the cage of one
Down below the sea is blue
Diamonds frame their morning dew.

Porn Star Therapist

Girlfriend; noun.
Definition: porn star therapist.

She throws her head back in the saddle
And neighs
Climbing up to his iced mountain
Then ruffles his tendrils as he
Pours pools of wilful woes
From his heart into her mouth.

~~Behind~~ Beside?
Every man stands a woman
Patting his back, taming his neurosis
Petrovsky can't go to the gallery?
Never mind. Carrie will drop all
Forget her dreams – his take priority
For she will ride to the moon and back
After riding him.

The world was her oyster
But she dropped it all for a chap
That blinked twice and called her pretty.

I'm sad, baby. Please help me.
Guys gain no comfort from brothers
Nodding and slurping their fears over beers
So they turn to us.
We're their saviours, their angels,
Swooping down to liberate mister misunderstood
From his many memories
That haunt and swirl the bristles on his chin.

Mother becomes girlfriend.
Girlfriend becomes wife.
And so she births and repeats the cycle
Of another porn star therapist.

By day, pray tell her your worries.

By night, mount her.
Let her be consumed by your world.

Give her the gift of knowing
She's not alone.
Sylvia ducked her head as Ted screwed sexy kittens
Squeals of 'Pet me Papa!' while Sylvia bit her mouth
And paid the feminine price.

Frida and Diego;
Two perfect
One disaster.
The minute he loses face,
He drops her, and she's stranded
In a boulevard of broken dreams.

Men.
Many men are beautiful.
But don't make him your dream.
Let him share yours
So you're not lost in his sad puppy eyes of oedipal longing.

For women are not here to be your porn star therapists.

Race, Gender, Class

Not everything need grasp
Race, Gender, Class
Sometimes a kiss is just a kiss
Sweetly plastered on a wrist

A brother can be a bastard
And a Tory is a darling

Not everything is about
Springy girls and louts
Let them play what they do
Treat me well, I treat you

White is not fixed
Spans sin, snow and Shakespeare.

Not everything needs to be
Brought to identity
I am you; you are me,
In this world we hold and see

Conversations with a friend
Are no means to an end
Simply cherish our bond
Respect carefree song.

Not everything is black
Or Jewish, this-and-that
But I do know this

Folks of any calibre
Treat you oddly
If you have panic attacks.

High

There is no greater high
than being desired by some guy.

Having him gaze into my eyes
                    like I'm a sparkling
                         butterfly.

                    When he holds me I am full
                         to the brim
                              with his
                              iced popsicle
                              dangling between
us both.

                                        .

Plunge your aura, ever fine
              and your seed
                    in my spine

for tonight, you are mine.

Why Her?

She's Vivian to my Elle Woods
A Jackie to my Marilyn
Peggy Olson to my Joan Holloway
Fish and Chips to Spicy Curry.

She squats; I shimmer
My skin is divine
Hair lustrous and curly
Twinkling its shine.

She squeaks in the background
Cute hamster on a wheel
I am the glossy brown vixen
Ready to swallow her whole.

She is your past; I float there too
By now I should be rid of you
Yet even when I lay in your arms
I couldn't help but wonder.

(Forgive me, Maria, this I do not understand)
Why I saw her smiling there
Skipping in the background?

(Forgive me my unholy thoughts)
Women shall not judge and scorn

still

We size up legs, lips, breasts
Us in the top tier hide chuckles and smirks
Knowing we're forever lusted after.

But behind the smug awareness
Of radiant, crooning lovebirds
Sad truth mocks our wings.

She may have been no Aphrodite

But she became your Cinderella.
Number one, I would never be
Even if you grew to love me
Because that spot had been filled
My chances, flown away.

Wherever I walk, I turn and see
another girl,
his first honey song of sunshine and rosemary.

How ought another fill the shoes
of a man's first love?
Her nonpareil toes snuggled under socks.
Can I compete with a year's worth of sturdy wear?
I ruin shoes within two months.

Shoes are adept to fit me badly
I buy new ones, hoping for change.
Meanwhile, she was sublime straight away.

Does candy walk on a stick
wrapped in shiny paper to be licked?
Does fruit salad surpass Tropicana Sunrise?
A nutritious meal, though less appealing,
more fulfilling?

These thoughts, they swim
(Forgive me, it's not my fault)
Eyes glow green into the deadlights
I see the face of It:
Dear man-to-be-loved
Running off with a woman
As dull as I am fine
His exquisite valentine

Why?

(Forgive me, father, mother, brother)
Shallow is the sea that befuddles me
I was born in a world that prizes beauty

Parading Lady Lovelies on a floaty plume
Her heart may be black, tongue spewing toads
But Evelyn's face casts ignorance on that.

Why must I drown in this reflection?
Obsess over high cheekbones
These pouty lips and doe eyes

Still, I rise, in wonder, no surprise
My loathing has died
Because for all this vanity and jealousy
I am simply afraid.

Afraid he'll never treasure me
Like he did her.

The Curly-Haired Girl

Tide washes away trampled footsteps
That dipped their mark in sand.
Pulling back, he lies, a still figure
Born of land, returned from the sea
By her saving grace.

Her song; sweet melodies
She lies above him, a little bird chorusing her message
(Pray, let him be saved!)

He looks up; sun twinkles his vision
But he makes out the curly-haired girl
Sparkling divine, her touch
A delicate feather on his cheek.

Who is she?

Words have not yet left his skull.
For now only her song enchants him
Glowing goddess of the sea
Fish tail shimmering emerald diamonds

Slowly he stirs, vision clearing
The curly-haired girl notices him start
To regain bearings
(Quick! Before the vision shatters!
Return to the sea; don't break the illusion!)

Back, she recoils to her world
Let him live his, and she hers
In his world, she is a siren
That glows brighter than the pole star
But in her world she is awash
With downtrodden clumsiness
Fickle flaws.

He is waking up...

Swim away, girl, before he sees through the enchantment
Swim back to the sea, melody
The tide pulls in, the moon's cycle ticks by
She splashes back to her home
Before the man rises.

Rubs his head.
Blinks three times.
Was any of it real?

Who was that mysterious girl
With the beautiful curly hair
And songs in this key of life?

Maybe she never existed anywhere
But in his dreams.

Time

Time continues to fade into itself
Once my friend; now my mocker
She scorns me, laughs at tomfoolery
Questioning; 'why lie awake and ponder?
Preen at the screen in loathsome hunger and thirst
Aching for a chance to dissolve?'

These pillows weep for me
Meanwhile I feel his hands soft around me
His face smiling perfect in my dreams
Bye-bye-birdie, she said, until we meet again
When this war is over
(what if it never ends?)

Can a person be replaced?
Replacing Barbara with Barbie
And Grace Jones with Gaga
One after the other; are these mere transferences
One set of limbs, longing and laughter to the next?

Hell is a ticking clock
Passing with each hour
Still she lies, her presence enveloped in white
Wails heard by no one
Until dawn breaks the slumber and she's forced to rise.

Awaken, sweet child,
For the terrors the night may bring
Will not surpass the day.
At night, you lie still in these sheets of pink warmth
With or without REM's descent
By day, scorn and envy and fear and frustration
Rampant from London to Las Vegas.

Does time matter or is it the consumption within?
Spend your days weeping endlessly
At night only to prevail and win?
Surely short bursts of passion

Hold nothing against years of love?
Or is desire all that matters
When asked by the clouds above?

Love and desire; she lay, a nymphet
And showed the boys the way out
Out of the black and back to blue
Until memories began to dissipate
And they were children again for a brief
Amount of time.

What is a child to an adult?
An adolescent to an old-timer?
Is fifteen months on the wagon worth fifteen years?
Or is it as they say; just for today?
Can a girl of twenty-one know literature
But not the sweet milk of his love?

How goes it, they may say
That a man once stared into the face of the wheel
That spun the hands of time, praying for it to work in his favour
And slowly, his descent into madness began
Until he had been swallowed and consumed
By this burning river of quantum light
Sucking all he knew away.

'MARTY! WE'RE OUT OF TIME!'
Don't we all wish to turn back time?
Goodbye, friends, hello again
When young lovers weep at the fall of the end
Only to return; bring back what once was theirs
But this time, it is fouler and desperate
She may have her youth but no sanity
So is it worth it, spinning the clock?

Time
Does her flower wilt or rejoice?
Sparkle golden silk or black dust?
Will we ever truly know?
How to spin this wheel of time

That waits for no human hand
Certainly no human heart
For the past is obdurate
Said the King to the curly queen
And it wishes not to be changed.

Not for you, for me, or for any in our range.

I Want, I Want

A veruca sticks to the sole of your foot
Chiming *'I refuse to go elsewhere.'*
It lurks and letches while your stomach retches
Seen the best of it; you have not.

Hear its cry!
'I want, I want, I want the whole world!'
It wishes to spread like a virus
Pray stop the beast before it swarms
Prickling pain upon pretty feet.
'I want, I want, oh I want it all!'
But veruca, I hear your pleas.

For I want his tongue to taste me again
To hold him tight to my chest.
I want his touch to pierce my soul
My shadow to gleam in his eyes.

I want my words to travel the world
Spilling yarns of grammar-gold.
I want tales and titles and Scherezade's crown
To ring my name in your home.

I want to tour the world on my guitar
Running stages from New York to Paris
For audiences to clap and cheer
My music enchanting their souls.

I want the world to be painted pink
Cats walking on hind legs
For the skies to rain chocolate chips
Money replaced by ice-cream.

I want everybody to hold hands
And clap till Zeus looks down
Seeing mortals loving each other
Hugs and kisses all around.

I guess I want the world to beam beauty
For there is so much beauty in the world
I want to grab it all
Paint a rainbow on my body
Hold a gentleman, bare our seeds
Together as one unified soul
In a world that reeks of loving warmth
Not bitter cold.

London Tonight

She whispered to the city;
It's you and me tonight.
Hold my hand, grip me steady
In London tonight.

A city crawling with life; vacuous space
Stretched afar from Hackney to Harrow
Big city lights, they fire up
Crackling the wind in its gaze;
Watches all the people as they turn Tottenham to Tottenham
Court Road.

Little people, bags slapping their thighs
Delights from Selfridges and H&M
Another Oxford Street Store.
Young boys getting high on the high road
Rolling their blunts, wolf-whistling at girls.

They say the boys are real nice in Piccadilly
But looking at them just gives me the blues
While the busker on the street wove melodies
Singing about the earnings that couldn't sustain his rent.

My dear, shall we dance tonight in Southbank?
Dance slowly in London tonight.

Four Times the Charm

Toad licks slime off his feet
Bracing eyes of opal
Ready to twinkle his silvertongue
And lies that spawn off it.

Ariel licks her innocent lips
And sits astride with a swing of her hips
But then she's ripped and cut to bits
By the toad's bitey teeth.

Build her a castle from country bricks
And bring a koala from Down Under
Sweet and fluffy and full of love
A new soft kind teddy bear.

Ariel holds this bear in her hands
But then he sighs and slips
Leaving her fingers clutching sand
And on her knees in bits.

Down by the river walked a giraffe
Ducking its bashful head
Said; hello darling, would you like some fruit?
Or a hat for your pretty head?

Ariel clapped her hands in joy
This was the one so dear
But then one day he galloped away
Watched by a field of deer.

Three times the charm, bye animal farm
Ariel's had her fill
She lay on her back and swore with a thwack
No more wildlife for today.

These flowers are pretty, these daisies dainty
Ariel knew she would find
Peace in the air, oh so much flair

For livestock of your kind.

Until one day she heard a purr
And saw a shadow breaching out.
The shape it appeared – was it a ghost?
No, a tomcat here on out.

Treading gently with footsteps, Ariel refused
To raise her head high and dry
But next thing she knew she tumbled and flew
Down into cupid's sty.

"What's different?" she wondered
"How can this be? This must be all a dream.
For cats are as sweet as koalas and giraffes
Yet disappearances made their beam."

But he rubbed his face against her legs
Insisting he was different
The perfect pet fully formed at the vet
Adoring this auburn-haired vixen.

So Ariel took a chance and allowed
Herself to be swept by his charms
She threw her heart out of her sleeve
And into his wide arms.

But once again, she was fooled and tricked
By naïve wilful care.
For the tomcat smiled then was on his way
Leaving her stricken and scared.

"How could this be?" thought Ariel
"I'm tired of all these games.
Once again I was fooled by an animal
That was cruel in all but name."

So time to walk on by and say
That this shall not happen again.
Four times over, no more heartache

Foolishness has reached its end.

If These Walls Could Talk

If these walls could talk
Watching as I tap my fingers over laptop keys
Untidy sprawl desperately leaking pen-to-paper
Wrists achy from guitar vamping.

If these walls could talk
What would they say?
Year after year, a witness to
my joy, hunger and pain.

If these walls could talk
Four walls framing a young woman's neon growth
(Don't forget the ceiling)
As she stumbles, drunken into sheets
Then picks herself up as she tumbles to recovery
A new leaf, a new boy in her bed.

If these walls could talk
What would they say to me?
Would they gush at my triumph
Or shake their head at my tomfoolery?
Smack their lips in disgust
And tell me to get a grip
Or gently cheer me on
As I navigate life's blips.

I Dream of Yesterday

Take my hand and glide
Away we fly, my prince.
Could I be your princess?
It appears not; so sad.
But alas
Yesterday we danced with no care in the world
No worries about tomorrow
Simply smiling boy and girl.
Yesterday the music was our crown
Sharply dressed; no need
We owned the dance floor.
Yesterday we gazed into each other's eyes
Time stood still as we remembered
The twenty-first night of September
Now it's March; and even though
I tell you my heart has moved on
I find myself still dreaming of yesterday.

Tiny Fish

The tiny fish swam to the surface
Desperate to catch the fireworks
That cracked their mass of colours.
She ached her little fins
Daring to get a glimpse
Of that enormous world above.

Below her; schools of neon life
Glaring golden, purple, orange, pink
So swam the fish beneath her
So sang the world above her.
The fish cowered beneath her gills
Her tiny heart beating.

'In a world buzzing with colour
Of fish that swim together
And the surface world;
its Dragon dances and drunken antics
How can I stand out?'

One prematurely grown fish
Whose gills are still forming
Tiny fins flexing their way
To the blue canvas forming
This vast wide ocean.

'How can I find my place,
When I am just a tiny fish
Hiding from hungry sharks and greedy divers?'

Infatuation

Arrow to my heart,
Pierced soul from tip-to-toe.
All so quiet, till you came along.

My eyes have seen you, burning bright
Hunger for love and passion, my quick fix
His voice is my heroin.

How did I live before you?
For now I cannot live without
The boy
If he does not love me, let me die
He resides in my mind
Ringing chimes day and night

Down she falls, rabbit hole of crazy adoration.
His number one fan
(Damn, girl, another man?)

She has been here before.

Over and over
Rinse and repeat
Cycle continues
Spinning machine, awash
Clones of her 'perfect' man
Upgrading every six months
Still the same idealized Greek god
Pertains her dream.

Dionysus,
Lord of Hedonistic Pleasures
The juice that bore my sins, rinse and spin,
For now
I win

(Not.)

In the end, screws in my head snap
Scattering everywhere
Leaving me in a bambling
Nightmare

While the boy blinks his eye,
Wondering,

'Is this girl fucking high?'

Dracarys

Burn them all, she said
It was a pleasure to burn.

Ashes of friendship scatter
Like strands of nicotine.

Once mild, now consumed by fire
Let it burn.
Hansel and Gretel once merrily skipped
Now hungrily devoured by the wizard's lack of mercy.

Burn it, destroy what remains
Our friendship became charred
When you declared me dead meat
Roasted and skewered on the spit of your words
Digital venom lashing out

So long, old friend.

Prodigy

I wear the chains by which I'm cursed
Of sweeping joy, relentless thirst
Conceptual sorrowful plagues of haste
Quickens hot pepper upon my taste

While fearing snatched precocious bells
Vulnerable child bids mother farewell
Leads one owner sprinting to stone
Who hits the wall with all they own

Crashing, o frightening siege of plight
Do tell these boys and girls goodnight
One pours desperate raging desire
That splurges upon this pointed spire

Tumble and spill like barren leaves
They spin and cry out as they weave
Magic carols, sparkling anew
Yet snakes they turn; tamed by the shrew

How does one deal with charming gifts
How does it, how does it, how does it glow
And lather up to Miss Bigalow
And chomp the trees up with its toe

How does one deal with seeds they sew
How does it, how does it, how does it go
Lock all away and brush aside
Leave for celestial sunrise.

7th July 2015

Edited May 2019

Floating Corpse

The water is my gravestone.
Overneath, I lie on the coffin
Body sprawled
Nothing but sun and trees luminating above.

Dazzle in the light.
Eyes close, body sinks
Forever, lay in this water
Basking in holy warmth
Baptized in the light of Ra
Beaming away my sins

Forever still, I lie, a floating corpse.

If I Was in a Wheelchair

If I was in a wheelchair
Money would trickle from the public purse
Spinning rosy quartz.

If I were on crutches
Crowds would part ways, no application
Needed to tend to.

If I had cancer
All would be lifted, accepted.
Common, tangible,
Easy to quantify.

But because my surface is
Pink rosy lips
Shiny skin
Bouncy hair
Crippled by heart not leg
I am pondered
Pausing, questioning
Printing and piling, pruning for proof

How must ends meet
When no one wants a loony on their team?

How must I break even
When I catch nothing from the office?

You say you want us to work.
Agreed; idle I am not.
But I would rather scrounge taxes
Than beg on the streets
Because no one wanted to hire a freak.

Catatonia shrieks without warning
How can I get well
When your lists are full?
How can I get by

When there's no place for tremblers?

Shall I let the scalpel kill off
Evolution's liability
Or burn houses and wait for the apocalypse?

Dreams

Cheering crowds, they gather round
The whirlwind of excruciating sound
Noises hurl and chant and bounce
Across the walls, the ceiling glance
In its consuming lair of white
Watching as I toss at night
Oh-so near and yet so far
I dream of a place that would quench Jafar
In all his heated plans of malice
Sharpen my wish with a cold chalice
Ensnared by traps of wondrous sloth
Clung to the window like a stapled moth
Fade in, fade out and daze away
As the words saw on harsh Monday.

4th May 2015

Hell

Ice burns hotter than fire
Feet pave harder than droplets
of pungent sweat, slapping with each beat
Breath so tangible it could be eaten
Doors creak against hooded hinges
Every last close, shut, open
keep the rhythm flowing and choking
Though the walls plummet deep in spine
Twist and shine, sing it now baby
Let the swing of this song commence
Whilst you're still young and innocent,
but a child of unsprouted flowers
risking all but to plummet in the sand
and rot forever like the grievance of new munity
hollow down in the depths of grimaced oil
until the pain bears no more.

5th July 2015

Zari's Dead

Zari's Dead
That's what they said
Let the folks run home
And see her through
But they couldn't make it
She knew what to do

Every bottle misused her
Ripped her up and abused her
Another girl gone
Drowning sorrows of old
Stuck in a world so cold
Self-pity destroyed her soul

It's hard for the world
To throw love in this girl
For many would agree
That her misery was self-induced deep

A Zari's in the hospital now
If you want to be an alkie, wow
Remember Zari's dead

Charities push for mental progress
But sometimes we must confess
In this boulevard of artist's dreams
Pure happiness, what does it mean
Ain't nothing to be said
Cos Zari's dead

All she wants is some peace of mind
With a little love she's trying to find
She could have such a wonderful time
With a wonderful guy
But she's just a woman child

Why can't the people
Respect all their equals

Dunking pills of age
Around the stage
In this day and age.

Tomcat

There's a tomcat watching me across the street
Sharp of eye, fur combed neat
He's got style licking from his paws to his tail
Smile turns upwards; playfully avail.

Yet underneath his jokes and mirth
Are secrets he may have held since birth
What would he want with a girl like me
Can his purrs truly set me free?

He capers and clowns about life on the road
Studying me; speech intensely slow
My heart begins to swoop and fall
As he slowly sucks me into his claw

What does he want, what does he need
Will his brooding ways grow tired of me
When a boy meets a naïve little girl
He carefully drags her into his world

His songs ring inside my pink ears
The sound of his voice brings me to tears
How could I have known he was a wolf in disguise
His smile never seemed to meet his eyes

Giddy was I under his swooning spell
Spinning me from heaven, then dropped to hell
Months of manic obsession about this strange man
Whose sins were woven by the devil's hand

You were a part-time lover, barely a friend
I was nothing more than a brief means to an end
Calm, collected restraint proved to be a mask
That slipped and revealed his empty flask

Am I the first girl whose heart you destroyed?
I'll bet the last one knew to avoid
Your stories of her didn't quite ring true

To my ear that sensed the lies you'd spew

Despite the wounds you stabbed into my chest
I wish you nothing but the very best
Don't cut your way into my life again
The pain you spat has reached its end.

I Need a Hero

Where are the princes I was promised?
Did they get lost in the devil's clutches?
I look around for someone sweet
Instead I'm splattered with sour cheek.

Where's my Robb Stark?
Riding on a horse; beautiful, dutiful
Putting his love over his land
With her till their last breath.

Where's my Jon Snow?
Brooding bombshell, kind in soul
No fake shallow wit or treachery
A true gentleman in blood and bone.

I'd settle for Jaime Lannister
Though one-handed he may be
That same hand fought for the woman
He loved and sheltered forever.

Oh Tyrion, dear Tyrion,
Please may you come to life.
Make me your bride, tonight
I know you would do me right.

Theon and Grey Worm,
Well-endowed they are not
But brave valour repents what they lack
Between the sack.

Dearest Samwell Tarly
Sweet, humble, well-read
Teach these lazy, foul-mouthed boys
A thing or two about chivalry.

I'm not asking for perfection
Pens are mightier than swords
He need not be Khal Drogo

Wielding brute, great force.

All I ask is for empathy
Sweet words need not suspect
Is it really so much to ask
To be treated with respect?

Don't tell me you adore me
Then throw my heart on ashes
Leave it to burn at Winterfell
Then disappear to Asshai.

Don't let me sing your praises
Dangling this sweet summer lady
Who simply craves compassion
I'm not asking for your baby!

If Lord Baelishs' of this world
And all the Ramsay Snows
And Tywins, Walders; Joffreys
May let themselves be known

Be-gone, you vile trouts
Better with you than without?
I think not; better off alone
Walk these streets like Lady Stone

For my heart deserves a lover
Who gives me what I'm owed
Not a man who makes me wish
Our paths had never crossed

A hero is what I'm after
A guy who treats me well
Not some half-hearted skunk
Who rapes my heart to hell.

Ready

Ready or not; they say
Are you ready?

Ready for love, at a time
A day at a time, one's love
Must come from within
Ready to share that love with another

Ready they say, you are not, little girl
Wise at heart, young of bone,
Still, alone, let it sew
Said the same things six years ago
Back then I longed to wring my hands
Now I sigh and shrug, wordless.

Are you ready?

How to ask if you're ready
To have a man's heart fill you with joy?
Is it wrong to desire love,
Not to replace, or to compensate,
But just to be.

Love.

Lovers in movies
Strike a knife through the heart
Sob goodbye as one drowns
Watch as cancer takes him

Their tragedy is my reassurance

Ready, never will I be, maybe?

Was she ready at fourteen?
How about seventeen?
Twenty; barely snogged the surface
Two weeks till twenty-two

Is it bad that I never made love to you?
But ride you I could

Why, I see many a boy and girl
Smiling deeply, arms skipping
Into the sunset
Two girls together, two boys forever
He is his, from this day until their last.

Hump him, I could,
Yet still
My lust cursed by a desire for monogamy
Each time I meet him he cracks my spine
Till I barely straddle the floor.

Do I overreact?
Am I lacking in tact?
Do I weep, privileged princess
Pruning curls, sucking cheekbones, smacking red lips,
Tight breasts, taut tummy,
Surrounded by ones who love me
Siting on the stacks of my success.

Am I ready to accept

That this is enough

And I don't need anymore?

Infuriating

Infuriating
I infuriate him
Politeness will do him no harm
Still, he's resistant to my charm.
Though I try to be astute
He finds me neither friendly nor cute
Instead his eyes grudgingly roll
Wondering how he got stuck with this doll
She's not cut for our pay roll
Better luck signing on the dole.
Though I tried to be pleasant and nice
He cares not for my sassy spice
Instead I am a disappointment
A liability, borne to cause trouble
Distantly spooning into daydreams
Why oh why does this grumpy man
Have to be so infuriating.

Wights

Blank-faced, they stand
Army of pale faced robots
Voices monotonous and dull
Eyes barely registering.

Discussing plans of worldly affairs
Concerning those at the bottom
Yet regard is minimal
For matters outside their hearts.

Everyone thinks poorly of them
These icy zombie monsters
I try being sympathetic
But even I can't ignore their flaws.

Their women gleam sunshine
Warmly taking me in as their own
But their lovers stay still and chill me
With a gaze of pure stone.

People are Stupid

People are stupid
People are stupid
People are stupid
Yeah they all suck

Men are heartless emotionless robots
Women are crazy angry drama queens

They claim to love you, really they hate you
Or they're indifferent to your pain

When you're unwanted, you feel ashamed
Foolish humans fill you with rage

No one remember your face or name
In shadows of superficial gaze

We may all fade into the blackness
Against a guise of false vapid screens

Quarrels against tiresome enemies
No one likes you if you're not on their side

Stand in the corner, watch the people
Tear each other to pieces over stars and stripes

While those on top rub their hands with glee
Laughing at human stupidity.

Chris and Littlefinger

Two sides, same type of man,
Flipping different coins.

Chris Moltisanti;
Hot-headed drug addict
Mouthing his way to success
Deep down, tortured artist
Drowning sorrows in distress.

Littlefinger; sly Petyr Baelish
Stroking his beard with silk fingers
Effortlessly running his mind over people's heads
Letting them play the game against each other.

Chris slaps a man,
Petyr sends his guards
Let them do his dirty bidding.

Chris knows he sucks
Self-hating cunt
While Petyr believes his lies
A gift sent from divine, destined
To have all clap and applaud his greatness
No matter the cost to others.

Chris tells me I'm shit
I make him sick
See his sins on his clothes,
Stench of cockroach grit.

Petyr? Merely smiles
and vanishes
Like a ghost he is gone
Leaving nothing but the memory
of his eyes boring into mine.

All the while caring not for my peace of mind
Instead, relishing in my agony

As I cling on to tales of joy
Imprinted within my taste buds
melting in my mouth
yet his kisses died on my lips.

Two sides of the same arsehole
Which is worse, I ask?
The man who slams his fist
At the table for all to see
Or the one who poisons his lover's husband
To start a war
Fist of fury versus skulking in shadows

Oh dear.

Why must I have such a soft spot
For rebels, bastards and broken boys?

Royal Babies

When the King lay with Queen Tabby
Babies were born of limbs and paper.

Baby Carrie; Mummy White cast
Her reign of terror guised as love.

Baby Danny; Daddy Torrance held his son
Told him 'run from my pain and be free.'

Baby Charlie; Daddy McGee protected her
From the hellfire within and outside.

Baby Todd; Mummy's Apt Pupil
Blind to horrors her son wove and heard.

Baby George; Daddy Denborough could not
Stop his son floating into It's mouth.

Babies stack the shelves of Constant Readers
Adorning tales that quench Annie's Misery.

Love and Desire

She came to each, one-by-one
Palm outstretched to try tenderness

Effortless love, don't be afraid
In the dark a boy screamed
In the light he moaned in joy

Her hair, Winter Fire
The flames burned bright
As her mark prematurely gnawed
The Circle of Twenty-Seven.

Seven Times Lucky
Round this circle, birds fly
Steady darling, don't cry
For I am here with you tonight.

Peace of mind, spread your wings
As he spreads his seed
Until next time, we shall meet
To defeat what nearly died.

Gleam and glow in my flower
As I'm with you tonight
Her love and their desire.

Blonde Beauty

She's a blonde beauty
Her smile wide and loving
Red lips flower passion
Laughs of pure sunshine

Yet underneath her smiles
And warm golden rays
Are chills of terror that purge her
Day after scary day

Her halo, lucid white
Shines ever so bright
But demons under her clothes
Drag her towards Lucifer's pit

Don't let the devils win
Your angels twinkle darling
Fight the evil with your soul
A heart of open love

When my mouth is running swift
And my brain won't stop the mess
Her words are sweet medicine
Tugging me back in check

We both fought off the liquor
Now we must conquer ourselves
Together we march through
This long night of hell

Don't listen to the voices
Spewing poisonous lies today
Remember you are beautiful
In every single way

You don't need a white knight
You are your own hero
Any prince would be lucky

To have you as his queen

And lucky is this writer
To have such a lovely girl
As her sister, spirit and strength
To guide her through this tough world.

Three Sisters

When will you three see me again,
In thunder, lightning or in rain?

I miss my three sisters
Zari's angels to the rescue.
Shine your halos of wisdom
On me darling; I miss you.

One:

Bitterness quenched my stomach
Now the acid has sweetened
For you I feel only pity
At yanking our history to pieces

Despite the pain,
Loving you will never cease.
When time is ready and ready is right
We two witches shall reunite.

Two:

Months without your gentle whispers
Buzzing in my ears
Softly did your essence glow
Being without you is tough
But avenues no longer crossed

Love you by day, pray for you at night
Without you, my dreams would not rest
In my hands.

When no one else could see
Your pen and love pushed me
Sister I can't wait
For us to chill again.

Three:

Now DNA binds us
Our father's genes entwine us
You are an enigma
Locked in fear

Sister, your heart is an ocean of secrets
I wish I could cut the burden from your chest
And fill it with rabbits, cute rabbits,
That fluff and nuzzle.
Your beauty is exquisite
Inside and out
Dear sister, don't be sad
The cusp of your children breed life
Into your soul
Medicine to clear a wounded heart.

Whatever storms come,
Or winds howl and hum,
Lone wolves may die
But our pack shall survive.

When will my sisters hold me again,
In thunder, lightning, or in rain?

Down Under

You and me made love down under
Oh, I want you to wonder
Your smile gave me a shudder
Down my back like a thunder.

August 2017

I Don't Know

maybe you're not ready

> you need to be proactive
> open Tinder
> delete OkCupid

> girl, you gotta stop using that app
> let it happen naturally
> guys only want sex

met my girlfriend on Tinder
two years together
worked out well

> "BITCH THAT
> NEVER HAPPENS!"

what is loving yourself?

I love taking care of someone else,
being someone's girl.
I do well wrapped in someone –

> else's shit!

relationships stink

> time for yourself,

don't think of it

> get it out your head
> you're

> too young
> focus on school
> career
> goals
> make dreams not diamond rings

68

(erm, you're happiness is tied to a man)

BUT he makes me happy!
dunno what I'd do
              without my partner

                        please!
        another person
        adds to your life, they don't complete you.

please love yourself first
this is time for you.

it ain't gonna happen now
take it out for a year

             love comes from within and shines out

      but I love love!
      to be with someone
      is the best thing ever

             but what about

friendship?

             children, families?

(it's not the same)

             best love is platonic
             starts at friendship

(unless that's all she wants)

he pined for a girl to take care of
they told him look for number one

come thirty? where's your partner!

so which is it?

do we wait, date, dance to penzance?

'Attention, do you have the necessary skill set
to qualify for a relationship?'

hold the door, questions cease to be

finite

but my fingers wish to sleep
so I ask,
and you answer
'I don't know.'

now let's watch TV.

One Hundred and One Damnations

Spotted him in the bar across the street
Looking neat; hands deeps in pockets
Long hair, plenty flair, looking dapper
Next dreamboat in line

As a kid, giggling at the boy in the playground
One handed over a love heart of suckles
Another sneered and grinned
Wickedly making my heart spin

Mr Man, hold my arm, I'm your queen
Gentlemen love Zarina
Curly hair, sexy chica
He'll come before he goes

Many many many men
Have lain in my heart and den
Spreading their seed, soul or scorn
Twinkling my private porn

A nine-year-old knows nothing;
Much less a twelve-year-old.
First kiss, I stretched up, he bent down,
Said it was funky and quick

At fifteen curves started to show
Hair donned scarlet gloss
Puberty kicked its heels, I was seen
On the dance floor; little miss starlet.

Eighteen and in full swing
Charming his knees to get weak
Itching to climb into me
One pushed till I succumbed

You dream of a white knight
Instead you get the black death
Marking his feverish chills onto you

Slimy territory no longer mine.

Alas; beginner's bad luck
For the circus spanned more kindly suitors
None sadly remaining for long.
Twenty-one, left wondering
If I could fill a room
With every crush, kiss, fuck and hitch
Holding my petite frame

Years of obsession blowing in the wind
Names fluttering around so frantic
'Oh, he's the one!' – I cry
'No, Him!'
My friends sigh at repeated antics.

Do I ever learn? Is this message received?
Or has it been deleted?
It's time to wake up, fluffykins
Too much testosterone spoils the broth.

Yes, bearers of Y chromosomes
Are lovely, playful creatures
Their bodies delight, their jokes amuse
For sure plenty will be keepers.

But for now, time has taught
That its best
To let sleeping dogs lie.
Stretch paws and tongues, and hibernate
So I can detox, cleanse and be free.

Plenty more fish surround the waters
The tide will never vanish from me
Just give it some time
(simply sublime)
When eventually you will see

That walking through the door

Bending to kiss your hand

Will be Mr Right

Not Mr Right Now.

Recovery is Complicated

RECOVERY IS COMPLICATED
RECOVERY IS COMPLICATED
RECOVERY IS COMPLICATED

Tell em, Kendrick.

Life Sentence

One small mistake
cost me everything.

Temporarily blew up my throat
Now I'm serving a life sentence.

No matter how brief the crime
The sentence is the same.
Can twelve steps to heaven
Resemble twelve years a slave?

Though I love thee dearly
My heart dances with gratitude
Lately I've been feeling
A solemn change of attitude

If I surrender all will
Am I forever sick?
Have smiles and open arms
Become my new fix?

They say this is forever
It's what keeps you saved
Without this life sentence
I'm down an early grave

But is that the truth?
Or does fear drive us all
Why not adapt these holy scriptures
To suit a modern hall.

Faith

"I've got really strong faith!" said the angel,
eager and shining with goodwill and compassion.
Her halo sparkling white
In her presence I feel heathen
Though she says otherwise.

She sings praises of her Creator
While I glower and wince
Unable to kneel before Sun-Ra.

But alas, celeste, I too have strong faith
not in magic, gods, incantations or crystals
Faith in myself
That light of inner love
Good Orderly Direction binds my essence
Allowing me to smile
and see

that your faith makes you happy
as mine makes me.

To Thine Own Self

Do it for all time, you chime
On this twelfth night of yours and mine

Everything these steps reap
Your veins, porous muscles pray, they sing

Meanwhile, I too reap the fruits of a good life
New love, our program beats as one
Yet our approach numbs.

You twinkle goodwill and love
Horror-struck by green of my eyes and smoke
Bespoke; that shall not cast aside my efforts
And you know it too

So why must I mirror you?

You seek not for my pink-plastered copycat attempt
Only my serenity
Of which you have gained.

But my love, our journeys digress.
Though we desire the same
Our paths must be littered
With flowers of different colours

Yours may hold a hubble of collective likeness
Mine splits across arbours of glorious plants,
Attracting bees all over.

May we both find peace.

It Just Is

Why is it that some people are so lucky in love
Moving swiftly from one partner to the next?

It just is.

Why is it that a man can train to be the world's fastest
Yet his brother takes the gold?

It just is.

Why is it that a girl will hit the books and study hard
Scoring C's while her lazy friend snags an A?

It just is.

Why is it that a man is born in a family dripping wealth
While millions making his clothes starve?

It just is.

Why is it that some parents helicopter their kids
Others let rugrats stay out late running free?

It just is.

Why is it that a girl is born gifted and gorgeous
Navigates the pen, stage and mouth?

It just fucking is.

Can't predict the cards you're dealt
Skull king, three blacks and a pirate
Could lose you points

While low reds and blues
Slyly rocket your score.

Your escape card is wasted

If you want that last trick.

Just because every advantage
Seems to sparkle your way
Doesn't make it so.

Everybody's got ways wishing for the greener grass
Stuck spending most their lives living in an alkie's paradise

But sometimes, shit don't mean shit
Just refill the glass
Neither full nor empty
It just is.

Red

Cut my skin
I dare you.

Cut deeply into caramel gloss
Or icy white hues, olive snowflakes
Cut our skin.

Out bleeds colour
Binding contract
Chemical bonds we have forgot

Blood.

Dripping to the floor
To the mud.

(Is this what you get for having a heart of fire?)

Red blood.
Red rum.
Pink flesh to rip.
(Repeat, repeat.)

Clone me and my kin
Let my genes mix with another
A man blonde of hair
Buttermilk blue-eyed bunny

Let our child combine us
Let their skin be cut
Shedding the same blood rippling through our veins

Cut.

I see no other colour.
I see no white, pink, orange, ebon.
I see only red.

Red is the haze of smoky clouds
Polluting Vietnam and Afghanistan
Red is the scarlet passion of lust
Hugging forbidden lovers

Red is the colour that leaks
when a depressed girl of any colour
cuts her skin

Red. Red. Red.

Pick up this sharp, cold knife
Its edge slick and fine
Like the glint of a shark's eye.

Cut into my arms, legs, face, neck.
This scar on my neck is the same scar
Worn by

Klu Klux Klan members and Malcolm X and Gandhi and Donald
Trump and Richard Dawkins and the Pope and Beyoncé and
Caitlin Jenner and Henry the 8th and Neil Armstrong and Jimmy
Saville and Mother Theresa and SLAVE OWNERS and
SERVANTS and CHILDREN and ALCOHOLICS and
FEMINISTS and NAZIS and CONSERVATIVES and PRUDES
and WHORES and GOAT HERDERS and SUPERMODELS and
BUS DRIVERS

Underneath our skin, we are one.
I see only one colour in every human.
And that, my friend, is how this poem should be

Read.

For more info about me and my work, visit the links listed here:

Website: www.zarinamacha.co.uk
Blog: www.thezarinamachablog.co.uk
Facebook: www.facebook.com/zarinamachaauthor
Twitter: www.twitter.com/zarinamacha
Instagram: www.instagram.com/zarinamacha
Music: www.zarina.bandcamp.com/releases
Music blog: www.zaridoesmusic.co.uk

Email: info@zarinamacha.co.uk

Many thanks for reading and purchasing.

Printed in Poland
by Amazon Fulfillment
Poland Sp. z o.o., Wrocław